REFLECTIONS

ON THE

GOODNESS OF GOD

TO A

NATION THREE SCORE AND TEN YEARS OLD:

A SERMON

PREACHED IN THE

FOURTH PRESBYTERIAN CHURCH, ALBANY,

ON

THANKSGIVING DAY, NOVEMBER 24, 1853.

BY HENRY MANDEVILLE, D. D.

PUBLISHED BY REQUEST.

ALBANY:
FISK & LITTLE, 82 STATE STREET.
1853.

MUNSELL, PRINTER,
ALBANY.

SERMON.

Many, O Lord my God, are thy wonderful works which thou hast done, and thy thoughts which are to us-ward: they can not be reckoned up in order unto thee; if I would declare and speak of them, they are more than can be numbered.—PSALMS, xl, 5.

We are by no means sure that the Psalmist, in this passage, has reference merely to those works and thoughts which place in our possession what we usually call blessings; that is, things agreeable in their nature, and associated in our minds with enjoyment. He calls them wonderful; but this is an attribute which may be ascribed to judgment as well as mercy; and to judgment, moreover, whether it be mere chastisement, designed to reform, and be in the end a benefit, or irretrievable overthrow: to correct and bring smiles at last where lids are moistened, and cheeks are channeled by tears, or to punish with ruin dire. When God removed Joseph, through the enmity of his brethren, from the embraces of his father, Jacob, by whom he was so dearly loved, and consigned him to slavery in Egypt, neither the son nor the father called the dispensation a blessing; and yet it was very wonderful. The detention of the Israelites in the wilderness forty years before they were permitted to enter the land of Canaan, was not deemed by them a blessing; yet, considering all the circumstances, it was very wonderful; and the overthrow of Jerusalem and the consequent dispersion of the Jews—a retributive and not a corrective judgment—was far from being regarded by its unhappy victims as a blessing; yet all who have read Josephus, will pronounce it wonderful in no ordinary degree; wonderful in fact, and wonderful as a fulfillment of prophecy. In fine, in view of these and other judgments, as well as blessings properly so called, the Psalmist might say justly, "Many, O Lord my God, are thy wonderful works which thou hast done, and thy thoughts which are to us-ward."

The text, however, contains one remark, repeated with variation, which presents the stronger reason to believe that mercies rather than judgments are referred to by the sacred writer. "They can not be reckoned up in order unto thee," he observes: "if I would declare and speak of them, they are more than can be numbered." Of judgments this can scarcely be said. Blessed be God! much of suffering as there may be in the world, it is the exception, not the rule. Men doubtless exist or have existed, whose pains through life exceeded their pleasures; but take the sum of mankind, take ninety-nine hundredths of men, and the judgments to which they are subjected, are few and may easily be numbered; while they enjoy blessings of which the totality exceeds their power of computation. Such is the goodness of our God even to a world of sinners; and in view of it, we realize the truth of the sentiment, which is certainly the sentiment of the scriptures, whether expressed there in definite terms or not, that punishment is his strange work.

Giving due weight to this consideration, we may be permitted to assume that blessings and not evils, mercies and not judgments, were in the mind of the Psalmist when he penned our text: "Many, O Lord my God, are thy wonderful works which thou hast done, and thy thoughts which are to us-ward: they can not be reckoned up in order unto thee; if I will declare and speak of them, they are more than can be numbered."

Understanding the sacred writer then in this sense, the text seems to us to express, gratefully and devotionally, a truth which few who hear us to-day can fail to perceive, applies with as much force to the people of this state and nation, as to the Psalmist and his countrymen, or to any other people that ever lived on the surface of this globe; and if bent to-day, as surely we should be, on making adequate acknowledgment of our obligations to a benignant and beneficent Deity in our state and national capacity, we can do no better than appropriate the truth, and employ the words which fall so sweetly upon the ear from the lips of the son of Jesse in the passage before us. To do this intelligently, let us consider, 1st, the wonderful works of God to us-ward: 2d, his thoughts. Our particular aim under both of these heads will be to impress you with their incalculable number.

I. The wonderful works of God to us-ward.

To aid us in forming at least a feeble conception of these, we ask your attention briefly to a few points of contrast between our condition as a nation at the present moment and that in which we were left by the successful achievement of our independence of British dominion in 1783, just seventy years ago.

1. Consider the difference in the extent of our territory at these two periods. The whole domain of the United States, or rather of the United Colonies, inhabited and uninhabited, in 1773, was bounded by the Atlantic shore on the east, by the southern line of Georgia on the south, extending to the Mississippi; by the Mississippi on the west, and by the lakes and British provinces on the north. In 1853, while the man yet lives who heard the proclamation of peace which closed the revolutionary war, these boundaries have been pushed at the south to the gulf of Mexico, and on the west through latitudes that include the fountains and the mouths of the Mississippi, to the Pacific Ocean. Ample as our territories were at the beginning of the seventy years which have now passed by, we find them, at the end of this period, speaking with sufficient accuracy, doubled. To say that this is wonderful, is to say too little: it is unparalleled in the history of the world. God hath not dealt so with any nation. Is it an unparalleled wonder as a mercy or a judgment? Men have not been wanting who deemed it the latter; who re-

garded such an accession of territory rather as a curse than a blessing. But their views, we conceive, were very narrow. It is much the same both with men and nations. If you saw a man who began the world, destitute of all capital except his wit and hands, in the unincumbered possession of twenty-five acres of land in ten years, and of fifty in twenty years, you would very justly regard the facts as conclusive evidence of his prosperity; of God's blessing upon his labor. No man who makes such accessions to his property, by which he can command the necessaries and comforts of life in abundance, will be regarded as unfortunate; no man whose gains are such will be deemed an object of divine displeasure. Just so with a nation. Increase of territory is evidence of prosperity and progress. No stationary people, still more, no sinking people, enlarge their domain. Rather they gradually lose what they have, like a man going down in the world, until at length, mere paupers, they live on the crumbs which fall from the table of their more enterprising and prosperous neighbors.

With this simple, common-sense view of the relation to our national welfare, of this large accession to the extent of our territory, we content ourselves. To proceed further and show how it keeps down the price of land in the more densely populated portion of the country, and increases the price of labor, and thus favors the elevation and happiness of the poor; how it offers a cheap homestead to every man who has virtue, industry and economy, and thus tenders a premium for these traits; how it stimulates labor in every branch of business; how it augments the resources and multiplies the markets of manufactures, agriculture and commerce; how it provides areas, vast and magnificent, for the foundations of free states, and invites the immigration of strong men, and much wealth from the old world—to show all this, as we might, would leave us time for the consideration of no other topic. We must dismiss it, therefore, to your own reflections; not forgetting, however, that this is the wonderful work of God.

2. We ask you to consider the contrast in population presented by the beginning and the end of the period to which we have referred. When the war of the revolution closed, our whole population comprised only three millions of souls, including slaves then held in every state in the union. The census of 1850 declares an

aggregate of twenty-three millions, and a fraction over; and at the present moment it unquestionably exceeds twenty-five millions. In seventy years a difference of twenty-two millions! In seventy years only! It is absolutely amazing. Language is scarcely adequate to describe it; nay, the imagination itself is troubled to conceive it. It is miraculous; as if the prophet's rod had struck the solitudes of this continent, and men had sprung from the soil of vallies and hill sides and prairies, every where, as waters gushed in the wilderness from the rock. It is a wonderful work of God! and what is the significance of it? Is it a mercy or a judgment? Of all the evidences of a prosperous country, of God's blessing on a country, an increasing population is the most decisive; and equally decisive is a diminishing population of its decline. When men grow scarce, you may depend upon it, labor meets no recompence and food grows scarce, and misery augments apace. On the other hand, if population is on the advance, you may be sure that labor is duly rewarded, that food is abundant, and that the people are in circumstances of comfort and happiness; and the more rapidly it advances, the stronger is the inference to be drawn from it on these and other points. What then, we again ask, is the significance of our unexampled increase of population, in seventy years, from three millions to twenty-five millions of human beings within our territorial limits? A wonderful work of divine beneficence equally unexampled. It speaks of plenty at every man's door; the most ample return to labor; bountiful harvests, happy homes: all, in a word, that can make a land desirable to live in, and all in a degree, that makes that land the dearest on earth to the native, and the most inviting to the hapless stranger, who, without being either a disobedient son or a prodigal, with every generous emotion of a man swelling, and every capacity of a man dwelling in his stalwart frame, and without leaving the shadow of his father's house, would fain eat husks with swine, and yet no man gives to him; tyranny deprives him even of this! But a rapidly increasing population is not merely an index of prosperity; it is prosperity itself; not merely is it evidence of God's wonderful work; it *is* God's wonderful work. Men constitute the state; men are its power, its wisdom, its goodness, and achievement; and that nation which has most of them in its quiver, and most rapidly produces them, is, other things being equal, most blest. If so, where is the nation on earth, when has one existed, more blest than ours, whose simple history of seventy years, by the wonderful providence of God, is the magnificent vision of the prophet: "A little one has become a thousand, and a small one a *strong* nation?"

3. Again, we should consider the contrast presented by the wealth and power of the country at the beginning and end of these seventy years, the usual limits of a human life. Our domestic and foreign commerce, in 1783, deserves scarcely to be mentioned; our manufactures comprised only home-spun and home-wrought products for daily and necessary use; and our agricultural labor seldom produced a supply exceeding the home demand. In fact, except in the virtues, in strong hands, strong hearts, and a sleepless enterprise, we were poor; so poor that, a short time previous, we had been obliged to go about Europe, almost in vain, begging to obtain a paltry sum to carry us forward in the war. How magical the change in seventy years! Our commerce floating on every sea; our mariners counted by hundreds of thousands; our exports and imports together, if we recollect rightly, between four and five hundred millions

annually; our tonnage employed nearly, if not quite equal to — perhaps exceeding — that of England, the greatest commercial empire the world has known; our coasting and internal trade unexampled any where; our manufactures, in numerous branches of industry, far exceeding the wants of our twenty-five millions of people; our agriculture with a capacity to supply the wants not only of our own people but of Europe; the wilderness converted into a cultivated garden, and incalculable mines of treasure laid bare beneath the teeming soil! It is wonderful, and, we may justly exclaim, what hath God wrought! wrought within the limits of the life, by no means prolonged, of a single man!

4. The contrast in education and religion is equally striking.* The problem of every year, from the close of the revolutionary war to the present time, has been how to make the provision for these objects keep pace with the prodigious annual increase of our population; and, considering that the provision for both must be voluntary, the problem is one which from time to time has filled many a patriotic and pious breast with profound anxiety. And what

* I should rather, perhaps, say here, the resemblance.

is the result which we are this day permitted to contemplate? Simply this; that our twenty-five millions of population are better educated, and more amply provided with the means of grace — with churches, ministers and Bibles, and other sacred instrumentalities — than were the three millions that emerged from the conflict of the revolution. There are proportionally fewer persons who can not read and write, and there is less religious destitution; while the state of opinion on both of these subjects — the degree of importance attached to both, and the degree of attention given to both — offer to our gratified gaze an almost infinite advance upon those of 1783. Among all the spectacles presented by this world since the morning of time, there is none to equal in grandeur, this! It is the most wonderful work of the ages; the most wonderful, with a national aspect, of God! Much has been said in Europe and much continues to be said, about the inefficiency of our voluntary system; but we wish they could show any thing as efficient by one-half. A system that provides an adequate, or even an approximately adequate, educational and religious supply for a nation doubling in population every twenty-five years, and at the end of seventy years provides a better supply for twenty-five millions of men, than at its beginning for three millions—such a system achieving such results, needs neither vindication nor eulogy. Its superiority to every other is as obvious as the grandeur of its efficiency is impressive.

5. The only other contrast to which we ask your attention, is that which may be observed between our present rank among the nations of the earth and our influence upon them, and our rank and influence at the period to which we have so often referred. Then, feeble as infancy, now strong as manhood; then despised, now feared; then abused, now fawned upon and flattered: then plundered with impunity, now able to extort justice and receiving it; then influential only as a principle at war with the despotisms of the old world, now towering and casting our spell as a mighty empire; intimidating the tyrants we could once only hate, and delivering the oppressed we could once only pity. This, too, is a wonderful work of God to us-ward. The change from the past to the present, is indeed so wonderful that we can scarcely deem it real. Could the man who died in 1783 rise from the grave in 1853, he

would be stupified by the spectacle of a nation awing the monarchies which, when he closed his eyes upon this sublunar scene, contemptuously ignored its existence or trampled it under foot.

But we can not dwell longer on these contrasts, though intensely interesting, and on a day like this, set apart for thanksgiving, singularly appropriate themes of thought. We dismiss them with two remarks.

In the first place, we have touched only on the generic wonderful works of God to us-ward; the grand comprehensive results. Should we descend to the specific, then, indeed, you would appreciate the truthfulness of the Psalmist in my text: "Many, O Lord my God, are thy wonderful works which thou hast done, and thy thoughts which are to us-ward: they can not be reckoned up in order unto thee; if I should declare and speak of them, they are more than can be numbered." What an incalculable number of subordinate works, individually wonderful, have contributed to the general and magnificent results we have briefly noticed! A few of these, just sufficient to send your thoughts in the right direction, may be profitably adverted to. And preëminent among them were the framing and adoption, as fundamental law, of our federal constitution; to which, under God, we may trace most of the prosperous fortunes we now enjoy. Next in importance to this wonder of the world, is the long train and succession of virtuous, wise and patriotic statesmen, who have graced the councils, and shed lustre on the name of our common country: next the tremendous wars in Europe, which, extending from the close of the revolution to the fifteenth year of the present century, preserved us from serious molestation during the most critical period of our national growth, and at the same time, by their influence on our manufactures, agriculture and commerce, provided the aliment of growth. These, coupled with the sagacious policy, first advised and enforced by Washington, and afterwards sustained by his successors, of standing aloof from the complications of European politics — coupled also with the contrast presented to this old world scene of turmoil and misery by our secure and prosperous condition, endearing, as it did, our country and its institutions to the common heart — exerted a prodigious influence on the formation of our national character and the development of our national resources. Next, we may gratefully notice the stream, constantly flowing hither from abroad, of wealth, but in the main, of strong men to make precisely that contribution to the industrial pursuits of the nation which its progress required. Then we must not forget the fortunate concurrence of events which led to our successive acquisitions of territory, to which we have already adverted; nor still less, the indefatigable attention given by our people generally to the cause of education, and by the church to the cause of religion; the one, the base of calculating activity and broad enterprise; and the other, their safeguard against perversion. Finally, descending to works less imposing perhaps, but scarcely less powerful in their influence on our progress, there are the cotton-gin, the steam engine, the steam boat, the steam ship, the rail road, the magnetic telegraph, and other instrumentalities innumerable, all wonderful, literally wonderful, combining to work out the astonishing destiny, surmised, but yet unrevealed, to which we have so far advanced. "They can not be reckoned up in order unto thee: if I should declare and speak of them, they are more than can be numbered."

In the second place, the extraordinary blessings

of the current year, for which we have met this morning in the house of God, to give thanks, though themselves wonderful, are obviously the outgrowth and accumulated fruits of the past wonderful works of God, principal and subordinate; and this fact we should not forget. Reason and religion alike teach us to recognize it on a day consecrated to gratitude. Let us thank God for the inheritance as well as the possession.

This ample domain, these happy homes, these harvests, these prosperous manufactures, these fleets and argosies, this wealth, this power, this national aggrandizement, rising upon the base of unsurpassed, nay, unequalled physical, moral, intellectual, and religious advantages, — are mainly the fruits of the wonderful works of God, in time past. With reference to most of them, we shall express all, when we give thanks that we have been permitted to enjoy them still during an other year.

Some specialities there are, however, peculiar to the present year, which we should not overlook. We should not overlook the fact, that, by the gracious interposition of God, we have escaped the very serious hazard of a financial crisis. We may not have even yet wholly escaped it; but the times wear a more favorable aspect, and we may hope the danger is now passed: a danger, the magnitude of which, they only can estimate, whose memory can recall the events of thirty-seven. We should not overlook the fact, that the past year has disclosed sufficient virtue and patriotism in the people of this state, to put down the audacious attempt of Papacy, to overthrow our educational system, and to change the tenure of church property. God grant they may never succeed. We should not forget, that during the past year the cause of temperance has gained unexampled success, in our own noble and time-honored commonwealth. The passage of the Maine Law is now, blessed be God, an almóst absolute certainty. At least, it would seem that nothing but unpricipled infidelity to pledges, given by senators and assembly-men elected, can deprive the people of its incalculable benefits. Finally, for we care not to exhaust the subject, we should not overlook the fact, that, as a denomination of Christians, we have been particularly favored of heaven. In unity, strength, enterprise, and appreciation, we are far in advance of our position last year. The church has emphatically awaked and put on her beautiful garments; and with God's blessing upon the future, we may hope she will shine; her light being come and the glory of the Lord being risen upon her.

With these remarks we dismiss from our immediate attention the wonderful works, and turn

II. To the thoughts of God to us-ward.

The propriety of making this a subject of particular consideration to day, or indeed at any time, if we would form a just conception of our indebtedness to a benignant Deity, will be apparent, when we reflect that every work of God is a simple result; and, however numerous such works may be or wonderful, they but imperfectly declare the sum of the divine cares for our prosperity and happiness. David understood this; and hence he adds, "And thy thoughts, which are to us-ward;" and it may be doubted, whether the language which follows, "They can not be reckoned up in order before thee; if I should declare and speak of them, they are more than can be numbered" — does not refer to these thoughts exclusively. Be this, however, as it may, the thoughts of God to us-ward are incalculably more numerous than his works. Let us consult our own human experience. Consider any given work of man; a steam engine, for example, or a cotton gin. As the former stands before you, you perceive the embodiment of one general thought, and one only; the application of steam as a propelling power. But how many thoughts of the inventor were expended on that engine, before it assumed the shape it has, and realised the purpose which it was intended to subserve! The work is one, but the thoughts which produced it, can not be reckoned up in order unto us; if we should declare and speak of them, they are more than can be numbered. Take another example: the successive works of an affectionate father, which bless the infancy and the advancing years of the blooming family around him. It is not impossible that you may be able to number these; you may ascertain if you count them, that they are a hundred, or five hundred, or a thousand, or a hundred thousand. Never mind the number; they are ascertainable and ascertained. But now sit down and count, if you can, the loving and anxious thoughts of which each of these works is the index and exponent; those thoughts that kept him wakeful when he laid his head upon his pillow at night; that entered into his dreams while he slept; that woke with him in the morning; that went with him to his daily toils in the office, the shop, the market, or the fields; that sweetened or disturbed those toils while he pursued them; that came back with him again to his fire-side, and that again followed him to his pillow: can you count these? As well count the visible and invisible stars of heaven, or the sands upon the sea-shore side. They can not be reckoned up in order; if we should declare and speak of them, they are more than can be numbered. If the child should measure his gratitude by what he actually receives from his parents, by what assumes the definite form of works, however wonderful, how unjust would he be to the beneficent guardians of his growing years!

Thus with God. His wonderful works to us-ward bear no assignable proportion to his thoughts to us-ward: his thoughts providential for our temporal felicity, and his thoughts compassionate and gracious, for our spiritual and eternal happiness. Many as the former may be, the latter exceed them in number, as the infinite exceeds the finite. And will our thanksgiving to-day be adequate if we remember only his wonderful works? O, no, no. Let us also remember how great is the sum of his thoughts to us-ward; those thoughts, so loving, and so full of care for us, which remain unspoken in the breast of a paternal Deity; the countless antecedents of his wonderful works. Let us *remember* them not merely, but endeavor to appreciate both works and thoughts, and feel the entire force of the obligation they impose on gratefully responsive natures, to love and obey and adore.

So doing, we observe in conclusion, we may hope that the same kind Providence which cradled our infancy, and fostered our growth, which has made our progress hitherto just cause of astonishment to ourselves and to the world, will still guide us at the same rapid pace to the exalted destiny foreshadowed by the prophetic past. What that destiny, ultimate and far away in the dim future, may be, what its grandeurs, its glory, we know not. But this we do know: that if faithful to our great trust as Americans and Christians, if we recognize God as the author and giver of our advancing greatness, humbly serve him, and make education and religion walk always abreast with population, enterprise, wealth and power, our progress will have no end. Of this, we are as sure as we are of the sun's progress to the meridian. On the other hand, we are just as sure that, if unfaithful to God and truth, education and religion, our progress will be arrested. The heavens that now smile upon us will brood with storms; and the very greatness that should have led us to repentance and made us good, will story the monument perpetuating the memory of our wickedness and untimely fall.

REFLECTIONS

ON THE

GOODNESS OF GOD

TO A

NATION THREE SCORE AND TEN YEARS OLD:

A SERMON

PREACHED IN THE

FOURTH PRESBYTERIAN CHURCH, ALBANY,

ON

THANKSGIVING DAY, NOVEMBER 24, 1853.

BY HENRY MANDEVILLE, D. D.

PUBLISHED BY REQUEST.

ALBANY:
FISK & LITTLE, 82 STATE STREET.
1853.

www.ingramcontent.com/pod-product-compliance
Lightning Source LLC
LaVergne TN
LVHW011139110826
845150LV00008B/2406
* 9 7 8 1 4 1 8 1 9 3 7 9 9 *